Where fresh and salt water will mix. We will jump

from the rooftops of the jeepneys floating. And end the day
going home with you having learned how to swim.

mpT
MODERN POETRY
IN TRANSLATION
The best of world poetry

No. 3 2023

© *Modern Poetry in Translation* 2023 and contributors

ISSN (print) 0969-3572
ISSN (online) 2052-3017
ISBN (print) 978-1-910485-37-8

Editor: Khairani Barokka
Managing Editor: Sarah Hesketh
Digital Content Editor: Ed Cottrell
Finance Manager: Deborah de Kock

Creative Apprentice: Chloe Elliott
Design by Brett Evans Biedscheid
Cover art by Honey Williams
Typesetting by Libanus Press Ltd

Printed and bound in Great Britain by Charlesworth Press, Wakefield
For submissions and subscriptions please visit www.modernpoetryintranslation.com

Modern Poetry in Translation Limited. A Company Limited by Guarantee Registered
in England and Wales, Number 5881603 UK Registered Charity Number 1118223

This edition is sponsored
by Arts Council England
and the Michael Marks
Charitable Trust.

Cover description: The illustration depicts the profile of an elegant,
dark-skinned Black woman. Her natural hair is closely shaven, and she gazes
towards the right, extending her view across the horizon. There is a coral-pink
sky, while she is submerged into a visually striking, intricately carved, dark
blue sea, with angular and sculptural formations that come up to her
shoulders. She has giant, white tears falling from her eye.

Above left: On the left, the Arts Council England logo curves around in a circle,
next to a black outline of a hand crossing fingers. Underneath both images,
'LOTTERY FUNDED' is written. In a line on the right, the text reads, 'Supported
using public funding by ARTS COUNCIL ENGLAND'.

Above right: An illustration of a crest showing a blue and white shield with a set
of golden scales; the crest is flanked by two golden lions, and a white bird at the
top. At the bottom, red text on a white ribbon says 'STRIVE PROBE APPLY'.

MODERN POETRY IN TRANSLATION

Fresh and Salt:
Focus on Water

CONTENTS

Editorial   1

KIM HYESOON, three poems   4
Translated by CINDY JUYOUNG OK from Korean

GONCA ÖZMEN, 'Say It's'   8
Translated by NEIL P. DOHERTY from Turkish

TARAN SPALDING-JENKIN, 'For the Sake of Strangers'   11
Translated by KATRINA NAOMI from Kernewek

NIALL O'GALLAGHER   15
Language Justice Feature: 'The Gaelic for "Apricot"'

DOROTHEA GRÜNZWEIG, 'Passion'   20
Translated by DERK WYNAND from German

NAAMA JUNG, two poems   25
Translated by the poet from Hebrew

VAIBHAV SHARMA, 'After the Ram Leela, a Ravana   27
   Returning Home'
Translated by DAISY ROCKWELL from Hindi

LINDA MARIA BAROS, 'Ode to elastic cities'   31
Translated by EMILY GRAHAM from French

RAINER MARIA RILKE, 'Experience of Death'   34
Translated by JOHN GREENING from German

PALOMA CHEN, 'Simultaneous Translation'   36
Translated by LAWRENCE SCHIMEL from Spanish

Focus

MELITA MATSINHE, 'Invite' **43**
Translated by BETH HICKLING-MOORE from Mozambican Portuguese

KIM SEON-HYANG, 'Water Snake' **45**
Translated by DARCY PAQUET and SUN KYOUNG YOON from Korean

ZAIRA PACHECO, two poems **47**
Translated by LAUREN SHAPIRO from Spanish

JAKU MATA, 'Before the City Goes Under Water' **51**
Translated by ERIC ABALAJON from Filipino

MAY MORALES DOLIS, two poems **53**
Translated by ERIC ABALAJON from Filipino

GUILLERMO RUIZ PLAZA, 'Chiaroscuro' **56**
Translated by JOAQUÍN GAVILANO from Spanish

MALLIKA SENGUPTA, 'I Saw the Ganges After a Long Time' **58**
Translated by MAMATA NANADA from Bengali

NNADI SAMUEL, 'Equidistance' **61**
Translated by the poet from Yorùbá

SODÏQ OYÈKÀNMÍ, 'river' **65**
Translated by the poet from Yorùbá

MARIE-LOUISE EYRES, 'Ocean Whirligig' **67**
Translated by the poet from English Braille

HAGIWARA SAKUTARO, 'A person swimming' **69**
Translated by JOHN NEWTON WEBB from Japanese

KINNARI SARAIYA **71**
'Grammar of Water: The Nature/Culture Continuum'

SAKTHI JOTHI, two poems **77**
Translated by THILA VARGHESE from Tamil

s. vijayalakshmi, two poems   81
Translated by thila varghese from Tamil

merima dizdarević, Excerpt from *far from the eye far*   87
    from the heart
Translated by jennifer hayashida from Swedish

rasaq malik gbolahan, 'a register of drowned bodies'   91
Translated by the poet from Yorùbá

concha méndez, two poems   94
Translated by harriet truscott from Spanish

nadia lópez garcía aka nadia ñuu savi, 'The Way of the Deer'   97
Translated by gabriela ramirez-chavez and
    whitney devos from Spanish

Reviews

dawid mobolaji, *Varieties of Space*   100
On Grzegorz Wróblewski's humorous, existential takes,
    tr. Piotr Gwiazda

jenny he, *Linguistic Dissidence*   105
On Yang Lian's political transgressions of language,
    tr. Brian Holton

Notes on Contributors   109

EDITORIAL

Our saviour, our destroyer, our own essence. At the tail end of hundreds of years of environmentally ruinous colonial capitalism, water is increasingly both scarcity and a murderous glut. As the climate changes, poems decrying the unfair systems controlling water, that have brought us to pain—like those of Jaku Mata and May Morales Dolis, translated from Filipino in this issue by Eric Abalajon, as well as verse by Sakthi Jothi and S. Vijayalakshmi, translated from Tamil by Thila Varghese—remain essential. The majority world speaks for itself, and will not be spoken for.

We are but water creatures, all of us, whether in gratitude for the Ganges, as Mallika Sengupta writes of a fisherman, in Mamata Nanda's translation from Bengali; in remembrance of the ocean's drowned in slavery and in migrant crossings, as in Rasaq Malik Gbolahan's self-translation from Yorùbá; or stunned by the simple observation of how the waves create their own 'Chiaroscuro', as Guillermo Ruiz Plaza writes in Joaquîn Gavilano's translation from Spanish. From Mozambican Portuguese to English Braille, from Japanese to Swedish, the poems in this issue originate in so many different linguistic traditions, yet were chosen for being, in addition to exceptionally written and translated, all deeply felt.

This depth of feeling exists not only throughout our Water Focus, but in the other poems here, including Vaibhav Sharma's empathetic ode to a Ravana in Daisy Rockwell's translation from Hindi, and Kim Hyesoon's ferocious poems in Cindy Juyoung Ok's translation from Korean, as well as in the reviews and essays you'll find in this issue. Each piece conveys writers' own exploration of their social and psychological spheres, the waters they navigate.

This is my last issue as Editor of *MPT*, a job I took on with the goal of shaping each issue as though it is its own poem, with the goal of caring for your work. In the last 16 months, I have been incredibly honoured to read and witness the contributions of so many brilliant

souls, each translator and writer a voice of passion. Thank you for the time you spend submitting, reading, translating languages you care about and are actually fluent in, languages that often raised you. Thank you for reading, for watching the videos, for listening to the podcasts, for joining the new MPT Labs, and for attending the in-person events when it's been possible. To the contributors, I will miss working with you in this capacity, but though I am leaving this position, I am not leaving this community. I will never stop cheering you on, wanting to follow your work.

We must never compromise, we of the majority world, on the need for safe waters, waters in which there is a true commitment to mutual respect between what we face and ourselves. I was the first Editor of colour at this magazine since it began in 1965, the first openly disabled and chronically ill Editor, the first Muslim, the first non-Brit. When we are the first to plunge into certain waters, we shoulder the risks of braving the unknown, violent terrains under the surface. I am sad to have to leave, but grateful to leave with my dignity, and with this issue—contributors, thank you for all your gifts, your works their own persistent bodies of water.

Opposite: In black and white, various photographs of various former MPT contributors in three rows of six. Below are the MPT logo and motto, 'The best of world poetry', and a quote from John Berger, saying 'ANYONE WHO WANTS TO SEE THE WORLD AND SEE IT CHANGED SHOULD JOIN MPT'. Below that is the ACE logo, as well as a line describing MPT, our social media information, website, and subscription info (£29 a year – UK Subscription, £44 – International Subscription).

KIM HYESOON

Translated by Cindy Juyoung Ok from Korean

Kim Hyesoon's 'Big Stone', 'Big Eyes' and 'Practice', all from her
manuscript *The Hell of That Star*, each use form and style to enact the
concerns of the poem. In the first, the stone that feels so physically
and mentally central, so defiant, is referred to in every sentence, with
the middle stanza further centering it with sounds and directions
separated into staccato beats and phrases. The motion of 'Big Eyes' is
in unraveling, and the mostly short, enjambed lines of the one-stanza
poem, holding together most phrases and clauses, help accomplish
this steady shift. 'Practice' revolves around the uncountable tyrannies
of routine and rule, and the repeating lines and words readily
perform this, while the predictable rhythm of most of the poem is
resisted in the last two lines. The parallels between the how and the
what of each poem indicates the poet's keen ability to bridge the
depths of any experience with its consciousness.

Big Stone

This damn stone that, if I close my eyes,
appears like a boss on a desk's
very center! This stone that, if I kick it—
ppeong—sits on my ankle!
The disgusting thing! I put it on top of my neck and precariously
walk   When it sleeps on a pillow like a boss

stone · heavy stone · big stone · dolmen stone ·
(with strength) Take · this · stone · and · throw · it · up!
Far dist   ant!
(as my face gradually turns red) Throw · it · like · a · discus · thrower!

Like my tombstone above me!
There are stones that cannot be hugged closely or trampled over
or chewed and swallowed
That stays on my eye like a stye but
presses me down more than an island: big
stone!

Big Eyes

As though unraveling
rolls of cotton cloth
unravel the knots in the joints and
lie the whole body down
to unravel it infinitely and
in the chest's valley
let the birds rest
around both shoulders pine trees chestnut trees
and cypress trees are made to sprout
by stretching as river water thuds on my face
ttuk! To flow out in a burst
To give birth suddenly to
a single sweetfish
To become the big eye that
gazes at that sweetfish laying eggs
with Pacific Ocean hurling
under toes and
makes the covered graves
pop from inside
out to throw far
Fat scarecrows
rising from under the flesh
high in the air
as high as the sun
To pull up
my aching heart
fluttering open
above the land mass

Practice

Each day comes and
wakes us up and
orders us to practice
There is a way to die like this
like this, to get up and stretch out
eat to fill and explode the stomach like this
become out of breath from delight *heehee* like this
in such hopeless conversations
cut off words in a moment just as
the breath is lost like this
There is too a way to die like this
Each day comes and
puts us to sleep and
orders us to practice again
While hiding a heart as indecent as that
to be mumbling words of blessing

GONCA ÖZMEN

Translated by Neil P. Doherty from Turkish

Gonca Özmen is one of the most prominent Turkish poets of the generation that began to publish at the turn of the millennium. Her first poem appeared in a journal when she was fifteen and her debut collection was published when she was eighteen. To date she has published three collections of poetry in Turkish and individual collections of her work were published in English (*The Sea Within*, trans. George Messo, Shearsman, 2011), German (*Vielleicht Lautlos*, trans. Monica Carbe, Elif Verlag, 2017) and Macedonian (*Не кажувај никому*, trans. Natasa Zabrchanec and Zvonko Dimoski, LAG Agro Leader, 2023). She has received many significant literary prizes in her homeland over the past twenty-three years. Her work utilises the rhythms of folk-music and is marked by a distinct preference for form and a critical, feminist perspective. She engages deeply with the Turkish poetic tradition but, by questioning its deeply ingrained male bias, she often ends up turning it on its head. Her third collection *Bile İsteye (Knowingly, Wilfully)*, from which the poem here is taken, was published in September 2019 to great critical acclaim. The volume is haunted by the expectations society places upon the notions of home, marriage and motherhood and how these then clash with lived reality. On first reading, 'Say It's' seems almost playful, full as it is of startling, thrilling imagery, yet a more careful reading of the poem will reveal a dark edge, one that raises as many questions as it answers.

Say It's

I'm murky somewhat. Say it's the Thames.
Say my mind shrivels up before a naked woman
Say I'm darting about among the llamas
Say my legs grew longer to wrap themselves around history
Say I found myself speaking a sleep-encrusted language this morning
Say there are two spirals on the red carpets
I cannot decide which one I should collapse onto
Say I rang you up in the middle of the night
Did I suggest we become more destitute
That we become more cowardly
Say suddenly everyone became the other
And this poem came in the guise of the owl

All day I was trying to pull up the panties
Of a word whose panties had fallen down
A girl with pink painted nails plunged her hands into me
No exaggeration
Out of loneliness I grew another tooth
No exaggeration
On a frilly feeling I remained suspended

Say the storks really did really did bring me
to this edge of the world
Say I made love to all twenty one by one
Everything was then left behind
moaning and stretching out
A road too had the right to cross to the other side
Say Ada walked along a sunken picture
Onto that enchanted scent that belonged to her alone

Say I sold myself to that abyss for a pittance
Say I skimmed a bird off your shoulder, a stone off your
    absent-mindedness
And matches off your absence,
Say for the first time someone walked side by side with me
To eternity
And for the first time I wrote lollipop-sucking poems for them
Slowly we began to resemble radiant things
Quavering things
A zebra darted out of me
It felt like looking down by night at Istanbul from an airplane
That grew and grew as it descended

TARAN SPALDING-JENKIN

Translated by Katrina Naomi from Kernewek

Taran Spalding-Jenkin is a young poet with Kernewek (Cornish) as a
first language. 'For the Sake of Strangers' concerns growing up in
Cornwall/Kernow, yet having to speak in English. I heard Taran perform
'A-barth Estrenyon'—'For the Sake of Strangers' in Kernewek—at a
reading in Redruth and immediately knew I wanted to translate it.
I've been learning Kernewek for eight years and this is the first poem
by another poet that I've translated from Kernewek to English.

A note on Glasney—for nearly 300 years, Glasney College in Penryn
was Cornwall's most important centre of learning, promoting the
Cornish language and culture. The English government forced its
closure in 1548, the college and its contents were looted and its granite
used to build King Henry VIII's Pendennis Castle.

Another note which may be useful is that red and white in 'For the
Sake of Strangers' refers to the St George's or English flag as opposed
to the black and white of the Cornish flag.

Taran's debut pamphlet is *Health Hireth* (Broken Sleep Books, 2023).
Taran, by the way, means thunder in English.

One of the joys of translation is being able to give another poet a
wider audience. Taran's work deserves this.

For the Sake of Strangers

I can't hear my language
I see my name
on the bills by the door
as if I'm not welcome

I translate into firewood
my voicebox ablaze
alphabet burning
like Glasney

I remember school
my mouth betraying
oppressing with its chatter
I smiled through the English

A road of dark hooves
resounds in my head
I can't think in my colours
only red and white

Opposite: a masculine presenting white poet tying their hair up in front
of a neutral background. Image credit: Sam Cavender.

Teeth fall out to this new language
the one pushing up from my throat
Lost teeth
scatter in the dust

I was made to call my Mammwynn
by strange names
'Grandma, granny, nan'
Words she'd never heard me say

This for the sake of strangers
So be it

Now I don't hear my language
but the traces remain
in my family's names
the names of our houses
and in our stories
of the land, which we Cornish built

And we bite the earth
leaving our mark with our teeth
for ever and ever

Yet our obituary
is written in your hand
Now I only hear my language
when I speak

NIALL O'GALLAGHER

The Gaelic for 'Apricot'

To be a Gaelic poet in twenty-first century Scotland is to write in one of the oldest vernacular traditions in Europe, to contribute to a literature of great richness and variety. The term 'mìon-chànan', like its English equivalent 'minority language', seems an impertinent and patronising misnomer. When I open my notebook, aware of the vastness of what's gone before and the infinite possibilities its blank pages present, the idea of writing in a 'small language' couldn't seem less to the point. What those terms do express is how Gaelic might appear from the outside, from the perspective of the 'world language' it lives alongside on a daily basis. In other words, though the terms 'minority language' and 'world language' don't tell us much about the languages themselves, they accurately describe the power relationship between the two. So, the questions of whether, how, and by whom poetry should be translated from Gaelic into English are as fraught as they are ubiquitous.

The prefix 'mìon-' can also mean 'exact' or 'distinct', as in 'mìn-eòlas', which refers not to the citrus fruit, but to 'intimate or thorough acquaintance'. My own acquaintance with the poetry of Josep Carner (1884–1970)—the 'Prince of Catalan Poets', for whom the term 'minority-language writer' is thoroughly inadequate—has become more intimate and thorough since I started trying to translate his poems. Carner's collection *Els Fruits Saborosos* (The Tastiest Fruits), contains only eighteen poems, but had an influence on twentieth-century Catalan poetry out of proportion to its size, and soon after its publication in 1906, came to be regarded as the foremost expression of a new aesthetic in the Catalan arts.

Most of the poems in *Els Fruits Saborosos* concern a single fruit.

The Gaelic language in which I write my own poetry historically assigned each letter of the alphabet the name of a tree, which I took as a good omen as I began the work, laying my Gaelic and Catalan dictionaries side by side. The titles of the first two poems in the sequence, 'Com les Maduixes' ('Like the Strawberries') and 'Aglae i les Taronges' ('Aglae and the Oranges') were straightforward enough. The poet Ruaraidh MacThòmais (Derick Thomson, 1921–2012), published a useful pocket English-Gaelic dictionary, which gives 'subh-làir' for 'strawberry' and 'oraindsear' (alongside 'òr-mheas', 'golden fruit') for 'orange', both everyday terms in the current spoken language. But the title of the third, 'Els Albercocs i les Petites Collidores' ('The Apricots and the Little Gatherers'), threw me. What was the Gaelic for 'apricot'?

If Scottish poetry is an ecosystem, then it is one in which at least three languages currently coexist. Since around the time that Josep Carner was composing his early poems, it has been possible to imagine the relationship between these languages—Gaelic, Scots, and English—as mutually beneficial, characterised by interdependence and cross-pollination. The Gaelic poet Iain Mac a' Ghobhainn (1928–1998), who published poems in English under the name Iain Crichton Smith, wrote, 'Let our three-voiced nation | Sing in a New World' (from the poem 'The Beginning of a New Song'). This ideal, pluralistic and cooperative, continues to pull upon the imagination of Scottish readers and writers. But it does so in constant tension with another force, characterised by the gradual encroachment of a monoculture, in which only one language—the English language—is allowed to grow here.

In the final decades of the last century, that tension gave rise to a debate about the translation of Gaelic poetry into English. Poets like Crìsdean MacIlleBhàin (Christopher Whyte, 1952–), along with critics like Wilson McLeod, became increasingly uneasy with the assumption that Gaelic poets should translate their own work into English if they wanted it to be published. That unease reflected a worry that by putting their poems into English, poets might render them obsolete, contributing, therefore, to the obsolescence of the Gaelic language itself.

Iain Crichton Smith's work suffered the most from the decision to translate his poems into English. This led to the disappearance of his Gaelic poems, which fell out of print while their English translations were republished, often without any reference to the Gaelic texts that had preceded them. Only recently have many of these texts been recovered and reprinted in Moray Watson's edition, *Iain Mac a' Ghobhainn: A' Bhàrdachd Ghàidhlig* (2013), which gathers together 331 Gaelic poems by this truly bilingual poet.

Iain Crichton Smith's might be an extreme case of how, under certain circumstances, translation might actually be harmful to the literary culture being translated from. The republication of his poems in English only meant that for decades large parts of Mac a' Ghobhainn's work were absent from Gaelic poetry. Subsequent generations of Gaelic poets have, until the last decade, been unable to read his Gaelic work in its entirety, and to learn from it. Iain Crichton Smith's excellence as a writer of original poems in English might have made the publication of his English self-translations alongside them seem attractive. But what made the omission of his Gaelic texts from new editions of his work easier to justify was the poet's own decision: to translate his Gaelic poems into English *himself* in the first place, to Gaelic poetry's great detriment. For the rest of us, it's a cautionary tale.

Today, while many Gaelic poets continue to translate their work into English themselves, they have developed a range of strategies to complicate the relationship between their work in Gaelic and English, so that the one can never be taken to be the equivalent of the other: whether translating Gaelic poetry into English prose (Eòghan

Stiùbhart), creating separate bodies of work in both languages (Deborah Moffatt) or translating under a pseudonym (Crìsdean MacIlleBhàin). The debate about the politics of translation *out of* Gaelic, then, has been highly productive. Less attention has been given to translation *into* Gaelic. Translating poetry from other languages is an essential act of resistance by writers whose languages have been suppressed, allowing them to develop their vocabularies in areas from which they have been excluded.

Paradoxically, translation can lead a writer in a suppressed language to create a text that is more *original* than a poem composed without a source in another language. A translator cannot indulge the temptation only to write about the familiar, using only the words that are part of the current spoken language. When translating poetry from somewhere else, words need to be found for the fruit that grow there. At times, that might mean borrowing from the source language, or coining new words based on existing Gaelic elements. At others, it can be a surprise and a pleasure to learn that our language has been there before, is better travelled than we realised.

Derick Thomson's dictionary gives the Gaelic for 'apricot' as 'apracot', simply the English word spelt according to Gaelic rules. As such, it is hopeless as a rhyme word; the implied plural and genitive forms, 'apracotan' and 'apracoit', even more so. Finding a Gaelic title for the third poem in Josep Carner's *Els Fruits Saborosos* would require a wider search. As Irish and Scottish Gaelic have grown from the same linguistic roots, I reached for Tomás de Bhaldraithe's English-Irish dictionary which gave 'aibreog', easily given a new Scottish form, 'aibreag'. The historical *Dictionary of the Irish Language* tells us that this word came into Gaelic in the Middle Ages, centuries before the development of separate Scottish and Irish written standards, through a translation. It appears as 'ébricc' in the prose text 'Togail Troi' ('The Raising of Troy'), collected in the twelfth-century manuscript the Book of Leinster, four centuries before the first recorded use of the English word 'apricot'.

So, for the twenty-first century Gaelic translator of Josep Carner, not a 'new' word at all, but one I might never have found, had translation *into* Gaelic not led me to it. The Gaelic 'aibreag' / 'aibreog' seems, like the English 'apricot', to originate in the Latin 'praecoquum', 'early-ripening.' Thanks to Josep Carner, Tomás de Bhaldraithe, and the unnamed author of 'Togail Troi', 'aibreagan' now grow tentatively on the branches of the Gaelic tree-alphabet.

DOROTHEA GRÜNZWEIG

Translated by Derk Wynand from German

Dorothea Grünzweig has published seven collections of poetry, including her most recent, *Plőtzlich alles da* (All There in a Flash), 2020, all with Walltstein Verlag. Her first, *Mittsommerschnitt*, 1997, awarded the Lyrikpreis der Stiftung Niedersachsen, as well as her third, *Glasstimmen lasinäänet*, 2004, appeared in English translation with Buschek Books as, *Midsummer Cut/Mittsommerschnitt*, 2002, and *Glass Voices lasinäänet*, 2008. She has also published a number of essays on language and poetics, as well as translations of English, Finnish and Wogul poets. Perhaps the most remarkable of these is her translation of and commentary on poems by G.M. Hopkins, *Geliebtes Kind der Sprache*, Edition Rugerup, 2009.

Drawing on her childhood in a Swabian Pietist minister's household filled with song and prayer, on her encounters with other languages, first as a student in the UK, then as a teacher and translator in Finland, many of Grünzweig's poems thrive in that in-between state, a suspension between past and present, silence and song, birth and death, light and dark, city and wilderness. Many benefit from the lucky accidents of one language's suggesting another, turning a translator's otherwise 'false friends' into true ones, finds of hybrid language Grünzweig delights in.

'Passion', from Grünzweig's second book of poems, *Vom Eisgebreit* (Icefielded), 2000, hovers nicely, I think, between those first knee socks of spring and the implied heavier woollens of winter, fairy tale prince and prince of peace, father and Father. It's surely telling that the mother opens the winter to bells tolling, presumably less somberly, as the father withdraws and the girls joyously swing.

Passion

The garden densely
hedged behind the
parsonage
its frothy
green first
kneesock day
went to our
heads
we build cloth palaces
between elderberry
branches wait
in pleated skirts for
princes to find us woo
us and meanwhile
wildly swing
to shake winter from our bodies

push off and fly fall
clamour up again and
notch a shriek into
the blue once at the
very top
we sling spring songs into
neighbours' hedgehidden
gardens

Then the window above
our cloth palace opens father
all in black summons us in a

quiet voice the sound
cutting us
to the quick
I do beg you children
sincerely collect yourselves it
is Good Friday the hour of
death come upstairs Behind
him we can hear
the dark cherubic rustling
in his chambers their
obscurity we see the
hand's stigma
and shame comes
        over us we have
given no thought
to the Man of Sorrows we
shoulder it and carry it up the
cellar steps then the handrail
steps into
the parlour

Mother by her prayerbay
window Bible slumping w
ounded
lamb blood dripping
from its opened page
father chanting bends over
it speaks sings the
Matthew text his torso
swaying consecrates the
sounds sparks flying from

his Rs his Ts' majesty
his sublime As and Os

We afraid because
raised before us the
swaying cross
Child sacrifice scripture fulfilled
mortification the Dying One's agony
father a wreck his voice at this ninth
hour
of darkness breaks crying
out for God God has
disappeared
death first raging
then soft
tranquility
There it is we see it through our
eyelash grid as if church elders from
the grave garden had appeared
transfigured
before our
flock faded
away

Defeat still hangs in
the air yet when father
looks up something
arisen in his eyes
victory plays in them we set our
gazes free smile tightlipped at first
then more broadly

mother staggers to
the window throws it
open
gulps down
light that bells
valleywide
surge toward us we copy
her already gardengreedy
father assuaged takes the
scripture up
and with a spring in his step
reconciled with faith and
children
he withdraws

Featherligh
t we're
swinging
still enwrought
we fly skyward i
nto the blue f
lutter down
and rise again
until our plank
seats with us still
on them release
from their ropes
first heading toward
the highest peartree
branch then blasting

NAAMA JUNG

Translated by the poet from Hebrew

I write poetry that is very concise and minimalistic. The poet Moti Galili said of one of my poems that it's a whole life in six words. My life is like a lab, materials from which I use in my poetry. In that I continue the tradition of one of the mothers of modern Hebrew poetry, Rachel, who wrote, 'Only on myself did I know how to tell'.

I write mainly about my relationship with my parents that was full of love, but also of pain. Some of my poems have Biblical, Hebrew and English poetry connotations, some are metaphysical. In the poem 'Past Continuous Daughter' I write about the pain caused by the absence of my father who was a farmer, loved the land and cultivated it all his life. 'Love Cadet' describes a hidden love and the frustration of love of a young soldier in the navy.

Past Continuous Daughter

I have a plow
with which to plow pain
in my father's
long-gone fields.
In soil heavy with separation
I bear seeds and furrow
words.

Love Cadet

I hide a small flame
that burns bright
within the darkness of my body.
Once I unfurled sails of freedom
but even then
a love cadet
I bumped into barricades
of blue eyes
that ignored me
at the control bridge.

VAIBHAV SHARMA

Translated from Hindi by Daisy Rockwell

VAIBHAV: This poem first came to me as an image. A man in a Ravan costume standing in a convenience store. He sticks out like a sore thumb and people gawk at him. So I started writing it and it took a turn towards the socio-economic condition of this man. Why is he standing in a convenience store? What does he buy? How does the end of Ram Leela affect him? It only lasts about a month. So I wrote about him.

DAISY: Vaibhav is my translation mentee, so I never expected to be translating his work myself, but I love this poem about an actor in the annual performances of the life of Lord Ram, the Ram Leela. Ravan, the villainous demon of the epic, is an ordinary family man who is himself a devotee of the hero.

After the Ram Leela, a Ravana Returning Home

After the Ram Leela, a Ravana Returning Home
Buys a packet of milk from the convenience store
and some bread
He's dressed in black, which seems odd outside the dazzle of the
    Ram Leela
as though a creature escaped from the zoo stands in the center of town
When he reaches home,his face smeared with make-up,his wife opens
    the door
Ravana returns home in the dead of night

When they receive their feast at the end of the festival
the children of the aforementioned Ravana give thanks to Lord Rama
Their father has told them to trust in God
(Ravana speaks Hindi, with a smattering of Punjabi)
Ravana and his family go to sleep just before dawn

He has not abducted any Sitas and prays to Rama each day
He only chortles menacingly on stage
Our soft-spoken Ravana loves his wife
and children
very much
that's why he strides off to do battle with his Lord every day

---

Opposite: a young man with glasses stands on a sidewalk in front
a shrub hedge with some trees in the background.
Image credit: Ashwin Rajeev.

That's why people watch him every day
like an animal escaped from the zoo
for a whole month
every year
until the Ram Leela is over and he returns home

The final milk packet will be purchased after two weeks
There is no pageant, no Ram Leela, on Diwali
Prices for milk and cooking oil have gone up again this year
but he's brought a bit of oil
this Ravana returning home

LINDA MARIA BAROS

Translated by Emily Graham from French

When in conversation last year with fellow poet Brigitte Gyr, Linda
Maria Baros wrote that her newest collection, *La nageuse désossée.*
Légendes métropolitaines (The Deboned Swimmer. Metropolitan
Legends), was 'not to simply revisit metropolitan legends [but to]
debone them in order to propose a new urban mythology, entirely
stripped of its usual artifice, [one] which is profoundly caustic.'
As the second poem printed in this collection, 'Ode to elastic
cities' is the first step to proposing this new urban mythology. Serving
as an introduction to the surreal, urban atmosphere with which the
reader will become familiar, Baros's voice breaks a city down to its
rubble in an attempt to reshape, restrengthen, and redefine its
legendary status by the collection's end.

'Ode to elastic cities' comes far too early in the collection for the
reader to make sense of how this mythology will be revived. For now,
we can only pay attention, asking ourselves every step of the way,
Where are we going? What will we see? How shall we eventually make sense
of it all?

Ode to elastic cities

Morning, like a crypt, walls up the city.
A tightly screwed vibration
   felt in the air's prestressed concrete.

Long boulevards leap beneath
    the banlieues' navel, dancing.
   Their comet tails and the clinker walls
   of tall buildings start to move...
Over the city warmly fans
   the facilities of la Sorbonne,
   the cooking of the ENA,
    where they boil students in cauldrons full of books.

But beneath the hotel signs — neon urethras,
   cleverly braided —, money starts to flow in waves,
    pulsing through the membranes, adorned in security.
   The city of concrete mates with the city of flesh.

The gaping mouths of the drains open up, released,
   under the sky, appearing as canal locks,
    as rusty sphincters.

In the parks, we hear a clotting, with a screeching
    of tires, the caterpillar on a branch.
   So arrive the roadworkers, stripped like composure
   on the police station's walls. Determined, they plant shovels
   into the earth, reinstating order.
     They ejaculate from the soil.

And the girls, they exhaust the curbside turbines,
                                             panting,
        as the tarmac rises in their arteries, dizzying,
                opening up the public locks in force.

This tender passage between two parallel streets
        resembles a nursing mother, her heart
        pushing milk from Rue Lauriston
                                        to Avenue Kléber.

        Sliding streets, immobile streets,
                the crossroad's imperceptible freshness.
You take your coffee on the terrace, in the sun,
                in the silence of your surroundings.
You are owner of this irresistible, elastic city.

RAINER MARIA RILKE

Translated by John Greening from German

Apart from the innumerable Rilke 'Selected' editions since J.B. Leishman's, it is the *Duino Elegies* that have most often appeared in English. But it could be argued (as indeed Michael Hofmann has) that the two volumes of *New Poems* (*Neue Gedichte*) are his most important work. A good few of the 170+ poems will be familiar because they are much anthologised—that celebrated panther, the carousel with its repeating white elephants, the women washing a corpse, and 'Orpheus. Eurydice. Hermes'. But the vast majority remain little known, perhaps because there are some heavy Biblical titles, and because they are tough nuts for both reader and translator. The poems of *Neue Gedichte* are often referred to as 'Dinggedichte' ('Thing-poems') because Rilke was applying techniques learnt from Rodin and trying to look hard at the world. In fact, not that many of the poems are really about things, but they are thing-like, beautifully constructed artefacts. Rilke was a painstaking craftsman. Rhyme and metre are crucial to his poems—as are word play and ambiguity. In translating the entire *Neue Gedichte* during 2023, I was determined to follow the originals as closely as possible, even deploying Rilke's metres where I could, but some of my earliest versions (of which 'Experience of Death' is one, written pre-lockdown in January 2020) were a little freer and departed occasionally from his patterns. Rilke composed 'Todes-Erfahrung' in late January, 1907, during a visit to Capri. It commemorates the first anniversary of the death of Countess Luise Schwerin.

Experience of Death

We do not know a thing about this leaving.
It keeps us in the dark. We have no basis
for hating or admiring, even for loving
death, whose true face is

disfigured by a tragic mask of madness.
The world's still filled with roles we can't refuse.
As long as we're concerned to show our fitness,
death will join our play, despite reviews.

But when you left, a streak of actual light
cut across stage from the gap your exit made,
a greenness that was actual green, a slit
of actual sunshine, actual forest glade.

We go on acting. Mouthing hard-to-say,
painfully-memorised lines, trying practised
gestures... but the fact that you have left our play,
your very self withdrawn at such short notice

can sometimes overwhelm us with a physical
awareness of the actual, a sinking close:
we play life out then to a higher music
and the last thing on our minds will be applause.

PALOMA CHEN

Translated by Lawrence Schimel from Spanish

Paloma Chen (Alicante, 1997) has studied journalism and the construction and representation of cultural identities. She has investigated the Chinese diaspora in Spain in *Creceer en 'un chino'* and has contributed to *El Salto, El País,* and *La Marea.* She won the 2020 Viva L de Lírica National Poetry Prize and has recited in festivals such as Irreconciliables in Malaga, Vocifero in Valencia, FuriAsia in Barcelona, La Voz de las Mujeres in Tenerife, Feministaldia in Donostia, or the Antiracist Culture Cycle in Madrid, and in spaces such as the Fórum Social Europeu Das Migrações or the Asia Europe Peoples' Forum.

'At a time when it is delicate to mention borders, migrants, and their daughters already born in Spain we've been tied to liminal spaces: those intermediary places, which don't belong to any side. Neither this, nor the other. [...] This poetry collection we hold in our hands is a reflection of how complicated it is to live on the edge, where traditionally art and culture have not had a place beyond the label of the alternative. Chen's everydayness, which spans from a restaurant in Utiel to a garden in Suzhou, reveals parts of itself, evoking different fragments of her life and presenting the complexity of maintaining a balance between all the pieces: the poet, the journalist, the woman [in] line in the airport, the one who doesn't understand, the one who yearns, the one who translates her parents.'
　　– From the prologue by Glady de la Cruz Juria

Simultaneous Translation

One day my parents arrived
and they found
a Spain that shouts:
The Chinese don't pay taxes!

....

1.
They ask:
Daughter, do the Spanish say that we Chinese don't pay taxes?

I translate:
No. The Spanish say that flowers grow on our bodies.

2.
They ask:
*Daughter, do the Spanish say that we're puppets
of the Communist Party?*

I translate:
*No. The Spanish say that as a people we're very
hearty.*

3.
They ask:
Daughter, do the Spanish say that we eat the dead?

I translate:
*No. The Spanish say that we're just lovely, not only
on the outside, but inside as well.*

4.
They ask:
Do the Spanish study the history of China?
Do they know about Mao, the Opium War, and the Last Dynasty?

I reply:
No.

5.
Don't the Spanish know
about the looting and the drought,
about running and hushing,
about spreading across the earth,

praising light and shadow,
building homes on the borders,
wearing disposable masks?

My parents ask me:
Don't they know?

I reply:

Y
e
s
t
h
e
y
k
n
o
w

of course the Spanish know that one is
more than flesh and blood

b
u
t
t
h
e
y
h
a
v
e
f
o
r
g
o
t
t
e
n

....

My parents
have
complete faith
in my career
as an interpreter.

FRESH AND SALT

Focus on Water

Above: Melita is a black woman, dressed in a short-sleeved batik dress, gold lamé head wrap and multiple strings of wooden beaded necklaces. Her right hand is behind her head and she is looking up to the right with a serene expression on her face. Credit: Melita Matsinhe.

MELITA MATSINHE

Translated by Beth Hickling-Moore from
Mozambican Portuguese

'Invite' ('Convite') is taken from Mozambican poet and musician
Melita Matsinhe's debut poetry collection, *Igniting dreams* (A ignição
dos sonhos). Matsinhe's style reflects the poet's background as a
musician and composer in attention to sound, rhythm and cadence,
as well as intervals and silence: what is not said.

   'Invite' reflects on water as the lifeblood of community, ritual and
mysticism. In translating the poem, I have endeavoured to replicate
not only the form of the poem on the page, but also the sibilance and
assonance used in the Portuguese.

Invite

From mystical
blood
and life
we imbibe.
Long live libation
of the sap
which spouts
a secret,
invisible.

KIM SEON-HYANG

Translated by Darcy Paquet and Sun Kyoung Yoon
from Korean

I wrote the poem 'Water Snake' after being inspired by Gustav Klimt's painting *Water Serpents II*. I was struck with how the women in the painting were posed in such a way that each seemed to liberate the other's body. When two women repeat to each other, 'You are not powerless, your body is free," only then is it possible to become 'no one's mother, wife or daughter', a 'woman of nature' whose identity cannot be fixed or defined.

Water Snake

In an expansive lake
A woman with gold-colored skin
Stretches her body to another woman
And, wrapped in water plants, makes love

Eyes fixed someplace faraway
Her tongue that flickers like a flame repeats:

I am no one's mother, wife or daughter
We are women of nature

In this place where not an ounce of weight exists
That spellbinding body!

A violent wave strikes the women
And at the moment of their climax
They turn into a water snake with two heads
And lay their necks upon the water's surface

ZAIRA PACHECO

Translated by Lauren Shapiro from Spanish

A vast, spare work set in a timeless landscape of rock and sand, the
poems from Zaira Pacheco's collection *Waking in the Desert* can be
read as a kind of origin story; through constricting the language and
the lens of each poem, Pacheco seeks to create an expansive
exploration of what lies underneath such limited modes of naming.
Cracks and fissures, pockets of shadows, and ancient water flows
alternately illuminate and obscure the traces of humans; heat
becomes not just the heat of the all-consuming desert but the body's
intense, overwhelming desire to live. In this landscape, humans are
animals, almost reptilian, and their flesh is like the flesh of their prey.
They are distinguished perhaps most clearly in their tendency toward
solitude, as well as in their inclination to name and thus understand
their world. Mirar, observar, ver—as readers we watch as the narrator
bears witness to an almost prehistoric narrative, deceptive in its
simplicity, profound in its implications. This idea of testimony, of
both experiencing and using language to reinforce what one has
experienced, is everywhere present, as is the emphasis on original
experience—the *first* fire, the *first* absence. We may not have been put
on this world to name it, but it is through this naming that we both
communicate and understand, in our daily lives and through this
very book that seeks to explore its own poetic impulse.

Nocturne

Once, in the beginning

you were time and quicklime.

You drank your thirst.

A serpentine movement

nudged you toward the first star.

You were sluggish, parentless.

You sat in your original state.

Steam ambling over the earth.

Opposite: a woman with curly black hair, wearing a black tank top, sits on a sofa, smiling. In the background are a lamp, a mirror, and what appears to be a window with light coming through.

To Be a Reptile

I loomed over the body of water

with a special thirst.

I sketched a mirage with my flesh.

The mass of my body

greeted its double

and drank of itself.

A cloying flavor of bison.

To return from the abyss always has its advantages:

To walk behind the serpents and their whistles.

To feel the wet earth under your skin.

JAKU MATA

Translated by Eric Abalajon from Filipino

Jaku Mata's poetry chapbook *Lugar Lang* (Just Land), is composed of
pieces that pay close attention to the culture and geography of
Western Visayas. This is done by cherishing intimacy while at the
same time being critical of the place's contradictions. The poem
'Before the City Goes Under Water' is a romantic mapping of Iloilo
City, one of many coastal urban centers that is vulnerable to rising
sea levels. As one learns about its streets and the rhythms of daily life,
readers are confronted with an apocalyptic vision where it could all
vanish. Mata explores place both as a carrier and a facade, of history
and of the future, of affection and of grief, and lastly as a refuge but
also a point for departure for elsewhere.

Before the City Goes Under Water

I apologize if I consider
the city and its establishments as my enemies.

But for you, I will set aside my
anger and bring you to its heart before the city

goes under water. We will start inside the buildings
where successful protest marches have passed by. We will

chase each other as fast as the flow of speeding jeepneys. We
will then rest our exhausted feet under the shade of the bridge. We

will consume history in a few bites of siopao.
We will greet the new souls renting the

vacant holes in walls that have lost
their former meaning. In city proper, the sea

has started to lick the streets. Flooding even if the
sun has been up since yesterday. On its last days,

I would like to gaze at my city with you beside me.
We will count the bodies in the bodies of water –

those who didn't listen to the visions of fishes
in the river. Where fresh and salt water will mix. We will jump

from the rooftops of the jeepneys floating. And end the day
going home with you having learned how to swim.

MAY MORALES DOLIS

Translated by Eric Abalajon from Filipino

May Morales Dolis writes about two disasters in Marinduque tied to
the Canadian mining company Marcopper. In 1993, Maguila-guila
Dam, a siltation dam, collapsed due to heavy rains and flooded
communities with water containing toxic waste. In 1996, a pit with
mine tailings had a fracture in the drainage, again causing release of
toxic material and flooding, ultimately resulting in the Boac River
being declared ecologically dead. It was only in 2022 that courts
finally ordered the company to compensate victims for the first
disaster, after almost 30 years. Dolis provides limited descriptions
of the actual floods, but focuses more on the aftermath. Literally
meaning 'what should be done nine times', 'Pasiyam' is a local term
for the Novena for the Dead done for a consecutive nine days after
the passing of a loved one. The author prefers to retain the original
title to emphasise the recentness of the disaster, which would be
absent if it is translated into 'funeral prayers'. In the poem 'Heap',
she contrasts the visceral experience of trauma by survivors, to the
superficial fascination of outsiders with the appearance of the toxic
landscape. Flood myths have framed people at the mercy of nature
and the divine, often one and the same, but Dolis lays bare the role
of the economy of extraction in disasters and the long quest for
justice that comes after.

Pasiyam

There are funeral prayers one after another in our town. One can no longer tell who passed away first and should be prayed over for nine days. The paths have become entangled towards houses with dim lights and dreary flower stands. The candles are confused as to whom their tears are for. Each family's gate is open. They are in disarray. Their loved ones have poison in their bones and it is spreading; creating a storm in the blood, and rushing up to the spine and brain. Delirious, their saliva merges with the bubbles in the shore, kissing rocks that turned red that eventually tourists would step on, eager to witness the tragedy of others.

Heap

Technically, this is a result of toxic tailings from Marcopper.
We can call this a 'beautiful disaster'.

from a Facebook post

There on the beach
our children took their first
steps, grew mindful.
Just like in any, in each part of the world,
we were sustained back then by water.

Also on the same beach,
us mothers were weeping
when their legs were cut off
and they lost their wits.

It is difficult to let go of what we carry.
The sand on our chests is so heavy.

How are you falling in love with this place?

GUILLERMO RUIZ PLAZA

Translated by Joaquín Gavilano from Spanish

You never forget the strange feeling when you first read a book that is not only set in the city you grew up in, but that also has a cast of characters who could all so easily be distant cousins of yours at a family reunion. It's a feeling that as a child I believed only people from European and US cities could experience. Thanks to Guillermo Ruiz Plaza, I too share that feeling. It is my pleasure to work so closely with his words.

For a writer from La Paz, Bolivia—a city and country with a long and complicated history with bodies of water—to write with admiration and respect towards water is, I believe, an unusual occurrence to say the least.

Living in our ironically named 'City of Peace' can feel suffocating at times. With mountains all around and an extremely culture-clashing population, there are only two things that are true for all Paceños: 1) we love Illimani, and 2) we all grow up without knowing what a clean river looks like.

It took me thirteen years to realize that the Choqueyapu River—the main river that runs all across La Paz—was actually our sewage system. We grow up being ok with that—we grow up thinking rivers should smell and have soapsuds naturally.

Choqueyapu, for better or worse, is still vital to our city. Without it, there would be no city. And yet, it is only outside of the city that it can clear and renew itself.

Working with Guillermo's poems has healed my relationship to rivers. I hope they in some way enhance yours.

Chiaroscuro

an instant beneath
        the moon
               where cloaked waves
reach like shadows
      across the shore
          then pull back
                  into their own
leave behind
     words on sand
        brimming with spume

MALLIKA SENGUPTA

Translated by Mamata Nanda from Bengali

Mallika Sengupta (1960–2011) began writing in 1981 and published
many books of poetry, novels, essays, and anthologies. She was also
an academic and a magazine editor. She travelled extensively within
India, and also to Sweden, Austria, the USA and Bangladesh. Along
with other poets and artists, she initiated Aloprithivi, a forum
committed to raising consciousness among marginalised women
and children through poetry, music and drama. All her life, Mallika
refused to shy away from mixing her activism with her art. She once
said '... I think a good poet can always insert ideology into poetry
without destroying aesthetic conditions.' Critics describe her as 'an
admirably alert, ardent and articulate person' for whom feminism
'is not just an academic issue' but 'a conviction and a challenge'.

The Ganges (Ganga as it is known in India) is a part and parcel
of people's lives in India. It is seen by many Indians as a sacred river
coming down from heaven to purify humans. Rising in the Himalayas
and flowing over 2,500 km through India and Bangladesh before
emptying into the Bay of Bengal, it is a lifeline to millions of people
who depend on it. At some places it is the source of irrigation; at
others it is a source of electricity; sometimes it's a sin purifier; it can
also be the destroyer of lives, but it is always a friend—a place to
come to when happy, when sad, when in need of quiet contemplation
or to cool down after a hard day's work.

I Saw the Ganges After a Long Time

I saw the Ganges
After a long trip away
When my eyes were thirsty
For something, anything
When I had nothing else to do
I saw the Ganges
One evening
Having been struck by hot air
I desperately needed to be brave and breezy
I saw the Ganges
And the king fish with wet eyes full of
Immense wateriness of the will to live
And an old fisherman standing
On the sandy shore, ready to go home
I saw the Ganges

And, I saw
How happy the old man was
On the laziest day of the year
I was baffled to see
How long and shiny it looked
The shadow of the old man's happiness
In the water of the Ganges—
He moved a little
Pulled away his net
Placed it on his shoulder
And, before moving on
He looked at the Ganges once more
And smiled

It was the smile of an old and tired fisherman
With no discontent
If anything
There was deep gratitude
As if, looking at the playfully drifting water
His eyes were saying

'It's getting dark
Dear water
Bye for today!'

NNADI SAMUEL

Translated by the poet from Yorùbá

An ardent lover of nature, I am a graduate of English and Literature
from the University of Benin. I am the author of *Nature knows a
little about Slave Trade*, selected by Tate N. Oquendo (Sundress
Publications, 2023). I won the River Heron Editor's Prize 2022; Bronze
Prize in the Creative Future Writer's Award 2022, UK; the Betsy
Colquitt Poetry Annual Award, 2022 (Texas Christian University);
the Virginia Tech Center for Refugee, Migrants & Displacement
Studies Annual Award, 2023; and recently won the 2023 Stacy Doris
Memorial Award Fourteen Hills), San Francisco State University
Review, amongst various awards.

The poem 'Equidistance', translated by myself, accounts for our
connection with nature—its carnivorous appetite, and how well it
shortchanges us. Here, we are at the mercy of the waters and all that
comes with it: both creation and destruction.

Equidistance

'It's the best thing I've found in 31 years of diving: the spot where a
centuries-old shipwreck lay hidden under the water for more than 200 years.'
— Maurice Belgrave

you can tell, the violence that keeps a boat afloat
has nothing to do with fuel.
your paddle of a hand worrying the hostile tide,
before taking the storm in one scoop.

the vessel— still, belly ovoid & sunken
till it leaks its way towards destruction.

kayaks cost an arm, to keep it well behaved in that polite wind.

you can tell apart risk-taking from its caretaker.
the way the second combines craftsmanship & luck,
rowing accident to acceleration— where
speed= Distance + the number of times the boat topples:

these twelve seething capsizings, like disciples in a water
Christ has been commanding stillness into.
a river is God's brightest trap.

Opposite [poet self-description]: Samuel, a blxck boy by heritage & not
complexion, stands on his veranda, wearing a smirk, white tee shirt,
head warmer and a slim chain hanging where a towel should be—across
his neck. Image credit: Bezaleel Photography.

you can tell, the way it mirrors wreckage & warmth,
consumes fluently a loin that torches,
sneaking luminescence into sullen deprived hands.

cupping a handful from the ruptured boat;
as if summoning evidence of life.
It's the best thing I've found in my 31 years
the journalist said to his colleagues.

and in the earshots of staff, blurted
How measurable is the wreck?

SODÏQ OYÈKÀNMÍ

Translated by the poet from Yorùbá

This poem is a translation of my own work originally written in the Yorùbá language. The Yorùbá language is my mother tongue and I speak and understand it very well. When I started writing poetry, I wrote in English, but most of the time my thought process is formulated in Yorùbá, because the metaphors and imagery employed are experienced in my mother tongue. Poetry in Yorùbá is called Ewì. The language has a rich cultural heritage and it's also known for its complex linguistic structure; tonality and extensive use of proverbs and idioms. Any change in the diacritical marks will connote another meaning into the intended word, for example, àgbọn is coconut, agbọn is basket, agbọn is wasp. It's interesting and it gives room for creative possibilities.

Writing this poem is a serious task for it requires 100% attention and intentionality with the languages. Some nuances are quite difficult to capture. The word Yemọja would translate roughly to a mermaid in English, but in this poem, it's deeper than that—it's spiritual.

Yemọja in this poem is a goddess, the patron saint of freshwater in the Yorùbá pantheon.

river

there is something about the grace of the river
that keeps me singing & dancing to the alto of her metal clavicles.

the rhythm of her gourd-rattle—the wavelength of her skirt.
but your uncleanliness is the broken chord altering the symphony

of this orchestra of godliness.
you who have made the body of water a septic-tank for your toxins.

you who empty your dregs into the belly of the river—
killing a thousand generations with your filthiness—

maiming the sons & daughters of the water deity. tell me,
what would you do to protect your own children from harm?

it is raining season again & you are praying to God against flood
with the excrement of yesteryears still on your palms.

listen to how the water laughs at your foolishness.
humans who have smeared their own riverscapes with dirt.

& what would you do without water? what would become of a child
without the amniotic fluid in her mother's womb?

this verse is a cowry of admonition—the dialect of Yemọja
telling you to treat water with dignity. listen: the same reason

you prepare indigo for your offsprings
makes the cattle-egret adorn her own with white garments.

MARIE-LOUISE EYRES

Translated by the poet from English Braille

I have started learning two new languages recently; Braille, as I am losing my sight, and Irish, as I'm investigating my heritage.

Above: early 50's woman with very short, white hair and a slight smile looking directly into the camera, wearing a dark shirt covered in angel fish. Image credit: pre-surgery selfie by Marie-Louise Eyres, taken September 2023.

Ocean Whirligig

The curdled outpour of local pipes
is whipped by tides into a froth
resembling a root beer float

makes an oily snakeskin across the surface of the blighted sea.

If you gasp into a splash
it feels like a punch, while
under the wave, near silence

a rumbling bubble of Hokusai turbulence

a salt-rich spin-drift
weighty with ice floes
and your ears pop

as limbs are pulled fast into the deepest chill.

HAGIWARA SAKUTARO

Translated by John Newton Webb from Japanese

Hagiwara's ground-breaking debut collection *Howling at the Moon,*
from which this poem comes, is a collection of relived experiences.
Each poem uses complex imagery, rhythm and syntax to attempt to
express the emotion, rather than the physical facts, of an experience.
The collection is structured in titled sections ('A person swimming' is
in 'A rancid clam'), in which the poems are linked by common words,
patterns and images, bringing out the similarities between and
particularities of each experience, and also showing how each affects
the other. Hagiwara saw and felt deeply the grotesqueness, ugliness
and seeming futility of the world, and this is the primary
environment of *Howling at the Moon.* However, he also saw beauty,
and was caught at times by the sense that there is more to life than
what we see, that there may be a God, and meaning, and the chance
for redemption. 'A person swimming' belongs to the smaller group
of poems which express one of these brighter experiences.

Hagiwara once wrote that he only started to understand his
own poems months after he wrote them. Writing for him was not
a rational experience, but an emotional one. The writing process
was never an attempt to make sense of an experience, only to speak
something of its emotional force. But for both poet and reader, he
believed that the reading process could, over time, yield insight about
the world. In its 5 lines, 'A person swimming' probes with body,
hands, heart, eyes and soul.

A person swimming

The body of a person swimming lengthens obliquely,
his two hands come together, and together they are pulled upwards,
the heart of a person swimming is clear like a sea jelly,
as the eyes of a person swimming listen to the resonances of a temple bell,
the soul of a person swimming watches the moon atop the water.

KINNARI SARAIYA

Grammar of Water: The Nature/Culture Continuum

Everyone is a born dancer,
Resisting pressures that surround her,
Like fish in water.
The inner ear still has the ocean in it!
We are tuned to receive sound waves through ocean. We are the waves
which have come out of the ocean carrying itself in the spaces
surrounding each cell. [1]

Kumar Shahani, *The Threshold*

Fish, adapted for the buoyancy and movement of water, began their venture into the world above. Through millenia, this daring migration set the stage for an evolutionary narrative that would mold our very essence. The fins that once steered fish through waves metamorphosed into limbs, with bony scales forming the knuckles and fingers on one side, and a soft, supple palm on the other. The nervous system evolved to mirror the branching of a river's tributaries and the roots of a tree drawing sustenance from the depths of soil—synapses firing, neurons communicating, mapping information across our body.

As Kumar Shahani writes in *Notes for an Aesthetic of Cinema Sound*:

'Both the senses of sight and sound, it may be noted, arose out of the need to perceive movement: to locate an object and one's own relationship to it; to gauge the pressures at work; to achieve points of equilibrium and to move in a controlled manner not only from static point, as we seemed to imagine in our classical civilisations, but to find in these different vibrations, and differences of pressure, the vitality of being itself.'

Amidst this transformation, we halt at the riverbank of being human, sitting cross-legged under the banyan tree as I am while writing this, like all storytellers. But speaking, not with my tongue, but rather through relays through my torso, arm, hands, fingers, neck, head, and face, eyes, mouth, eyebrows... a gestural lexicon signaling the cascading beats of my core – slapping on our bellies or chest to drum before skins were stretched to make drums. Our bodies become the living verses of timeless gestures, in the poetry of our existence.

As a dancer trained in India, I was taught to move in jagged, serpentine lines like twisted branches. Our limbs were trained at a young age to stretch the ligaments of joints so that bodies can flow like the curves of a river to evade the rational will of a straight line.

It is an invocation for us to find circularity in the curves and repetitive imbalances of the dancer's metric timekeeping of 16 taals (beats). The 16 taals are slowed down, stretched, sped up, and compressed to forge fractals of gestures, a sequence of laya (rhythm), emotions and impulses which nurture the body and to which it returns.

In Indian music and dance, a taal is a poetic structure that follows a cyclic rhythm. After varying in intensity across the remaining 15 beats, it always faithfully returns back to its first. Each taal contains 'claps' and 'waves' that denote which beats are stressed (the claps) and unstressed (the waves), marked on the soft side of the palm. In Teentaal (16 taals), for instance, claps are on beats 1, 5 and 13, with 9 as a wave, an audible emptiness. In this dance, the claps and waves that punctuate the taal become the punctuation marks of a poetry in motion. The claps are the exclamation points, emphasizing the beats

Opposite: an Indian woman with long hair, glasses, and a patterned, sleeveless dress looks into the camera.

with vigor and intensity. The waves, on the other hand, become the spaces between words, allowing emotions to breathe, like the commas and semicolons that shape the flow of a poem.

For a rhythm to occur, the continuous duration must be interrupted, and it must return and continue so that it can be interrupted again. Similarly, water has its own laya (rhythm), existing in taals (beats) of seasonal oscillations between high waters, falling waters, low waters and rising waters, that repeat, return and revolve around each other in the process of their own disappearance.

In the depths of the ocean, where light dissipates into shadows, the interruption and return of clicks, pulses and the audible emptiness is what allows whales 'to locate an object' and find their 'own relationship to it'. By emitting high-frequency clicks and listening intently to the returning echoes, whales form fractals of information constellating in a terrestrial map of the underwater. Much like the beats of a taal, these acoustic pulses are modulated – slowed down, stretched, sped up, and compressed – for whales 'to move in a controlled manner not only from static point, but to find in these different vibrations, and differences of pressure, the vitality of being itself'.

Whales evolved to lose emphasis on vision and develop echolocation when they left behind terra firma. But their tail, as they propel through the ocean, still carries traces of their ancient, terrestrial heritage. To swim, they dance their tails up and down, rather than back and forth as fishes do. This biomechanical inheritance comes from their land-dwelling ancestors, whose backbones did not naturally bend side to side, but up and down. A whale's vertebral column undulates up and down in waves as it moves forward.

The rhythmic oscillation of senses, as creatures evolve from land to water and back again, are submerged in the way our bodies move through the world. This convergence of past and present in ephemeral performative practice is always in transition, from one beat to another, from one hand gesture to another, from one species to another, before returning back to its first iteration to begin the journey all over again. These drummings, cries, crawls, highs and lows, meanders, body lines moving like a droplet on a spider's silk thread or a whirlpool's eye, all intimate a matrix of vital signs that await our ability to hear the water's call. To feel in its vibration and pulse, as it curves uninterrupted, the rhythms that inform dance-making as poetry-making.

Above: a woman with long, black hair, smiling to the camera, against an outdoors background with greenery. She is wearing jewellery and a sari.

SAKTHI JOTHI

Translated by Thila Varghese from Tamil

In her poem 'Water', Sakthi Jothi captures the grim reality of fresh water scarcity. As water, one of the basic human needs for survival, continues to dwindle, the desperate search for water is set in motion. The narrator in the poem runs 'twelve miles' and could only find 'three earthenware pitchers' of water, not enough to quench the thirst. A far and wide search results in just 'a spoonful' of liquid from inside a palm fruit and 'a pitcher full of water' from a clear stream. The narrator then turns to the rivers for more water, but 'they are waiting for the rain.' While everyone anxiously waits fresh water, the gravity of the situation is further aggravated by the seas engulfing everything.

As if lack of fresh water is not bad enough, ongoing sand excavation in river beds pose additional threat to biodiversity and ecosystem as presented in Sakthi Jothi's poem 'The River Devoid of Sand'. A riverside bustling with communal activities involving the young and the old alike, and all living creatures, is deserted at the sound of the 'yellow lorries' that arrive 'howling like giants' to haul from riverbeds huge quantities of sand, in which 'small snails curl up and die'. The poet deplores the indiscriminate hauling of sand for commercial purposes, which not only depletes nutrients and life forms from the riverside but also negatively impacts the natural water recharge, further reducing access to the precious resource.

Water

They said
they wanted water;
I ran twelve miles.
Drinking three earthenware pitchers
of water was not enough,
so I started roaming far and wide
in search of water.

I looked for it inside the palm fruit;
a spoonful was obtained.
In a clear stream,
I managed to scoop out
a pitcher full of water.
Even that was not enough,
so I turned to the rivers;
they were waiting for the rain.

The clouds
were calm.
The wind
was tight-lipped.
The land
remained silent.
While the world
awaited fresh water,
the oceans
engulfed
everything.

The River Devoid of Sand

Someone has uprooted
and tossed aside
the plants
we had planted
on the riverside.

Missing
are the pebbles
we had kept aside
for thattaangal game.

The elderly who feed
puffed rice to baby fish
didn't come today.

The little girls
who scoop out water
from underneath the sand
for fun
run away terrified.

Howling like giant wolves
arrive the yellow lorries.

About to crash down
in just a few minutes
are the neem trees we use
for drying our washed clothes.

Inside the dug-out sand
that the lorries haul,
small snails
curl up and die.

S. VIJAYALAKSHMI

Translated by Thila Varghese from Tamil

In her poem 'Beauty', poet Vijayalakshmi brings attention to the
dried-up riverbeds devoid of water, and fast forwards to a time 'when
the land looks pale like a sick woman' having lost its natural beauty,
at which time only photographs will have to be used to show for
posterity what it was like when floodwater overflowed. With rivers,
shores, and the forests reduced to concrete buildings, produce is
grown in terrace gardens and 'groceries are delivered by drone'.
The almanac predictions of rains are short-lived while foreign
companies claim even the limited amount of deep bore well water
for commercial purposes. The poet laments over the scenario in
which the beauty of the land and the evergreen landscape of
yesteryears can only be seen on paper.

In 'Sempeyal', Vijayalakshmi presents an alternate picture
of a 'healthy' land that receives the seasonal rains it yearns for, both
for its productivity and the well-being of all living things. The
ritualistic preparations of getting the paddy seeds ready for the fields
followed by the much-awaited monsoons, the landscape transforms
into a glorious celebration of nature as 'the enormous flow of heavy
rainfall inextricably blends with fine rich reddish soil' like a man
and woman bound together in love.

Beauty

At a time
when the land
looks pale
like a sick woman,
with dried up rivers,
devoid of
quarried out
riverbed sand,
and prevalent mirages,
we could show the photographs
and say,
'Look, this is how
the flood overflowed.'

Where are the rivers?
Where are the shores?
Where are the forests?
Everything reduced to
barren hard soil
and concrete buildings.

We cooked drumsticks and chillies
grown in our terrace gardens

Opposite: a woman smiling and looking beyond the camera, against a
grey background. She has long, black hair tied back, and silver jewellery,
wearing a sari.

while groceries are delivered
by drone
to our neighbour Bhargavi's home.

Whether almanac predictions
come true or not,

the forecasted rains, rivers,
and water supplies
remain short-lived.
'That is world politics', said someone.
'Hey,
Let's save the water that falls
and then talk politics', said a wayfarer.

Deep bore well water
yielded six hundred litres.
Even those
are pumped out and sold
by only foreign companies.
Meanwhile,
the beauty of nature
and Sangam Age land divisions,
—mountain areas,
forest regions,
paddy field landscapes
and localities related to oceans—
are seen as
chlorophyll pigments
only to be seen on paper.

Sempeyal

She looked at him deeply;
an aloe vera split open.
With his hand,
he searched for the grains
inside the pot in which
Kattuyanam red rice was stored.
He took out some grains
and, rubbing them in the palm of his hand,
he put them in his mouth.
The taste of the grains
unfolded inside
the corner of his cheeks.
In the water that burst out of aloe vera,
he mixed the Kattuyanam grains.
With the paddy seeds
heaped on the ground,
the grain pot
was placed
on the top of the heap
as a kalasam,
the crowning ornament.

The monsoon season
in the offing,
the living creatures
and the forest terrain
yearned for the rivers of the forest.

As it thundered,
torrential rains
flooding the forest river
morphed into an enormous flow
of sempeyal,
the heavy rainfall
inextricably blended with
fine rich reddish soil.

MERIMA DIZDAREVIĆ

Translated by Jennifer Hayashida from Swedish

Merima Dizdarević's debut collection *far from the eye far from the heart* (Albert Bonniers förlag, 2022) is a vertiginous and exorcising excavation of memory in the aftermath of war, forced displacement, and return. The book's polyvocal poetics act as a vessel that continuously springs leaks, and in that leakage frees itself from the dictates of form, genre, or the lyric. Diaspora, here, becomes shrapnel lodged in tongue and heart, ballast seeds scattered through involuntary transport and translated into invasive species.

Organized into six sections, the collection sprints and falters in a narrative syncopation, imagining and staging a critical poetics of a poet-witness in perpetual motion. At times, it is as though the poems hurtle across themselves in movements between and across languages and genres, where the smooth terrain of the idiomatic often turns rocky in flux. If the poet is both gleaner and seafarer, the book suggests, how is the poem simultaneously salt in a thousand wounds as well as a curative—a brine for preserving what has been lost over and over again?

Excerpt from *far from the eye far from the heart*

I dreamt of a waterfall
       I was told
I dreamt of it in detail but
had not been there since I was little
distances then so vast
one day when I was eighteen I was nearby and went there
I was speechless when I stood in front of it
it was precisely the waterfall I had dreamt of
I stood there and looked at it
then
two seagulls flew past above me and
I closed my eyes and realized that I would die
I had known even earlier but
it was then I truly understood
and
with that
I could begin to live

Opposite: headshot of a feminine-presenting person with long hair,
wearing a black shirt and blazer, against a dark background.
Photo credit: David Möller.

Above: The poet wearing a dark pair of glasses while leaning against the wall in his room.

RASAQ MALIK GBOLAHAN

Translated by the poet from Yorùbá

'a register of drowned bodies' is a memorial for those lost to the precarious world of the sea. It explores the harrowing experiences of crossing the sea and the fragility of life rooted in the body of water. Tracing the haunting event of the Igbo landing and rendering it through the grim realities surrounding the sea, the poem offers ways of thinking about the gory past and the inerasable traces of slavery— especially the middle passage and memories of slaves ferried to a new land to be sold into slavery. While grieving the losses at sea, the poem also celebrates the spirit of revolt exhibited by the Igbo slaves and their courage in the face of the grim reality of drowning. In addition to the event of the Igbo landing, the poem connects us to the exodus happening daily in countries across the world and the unsafe lives of those fleeing war-torn homelands—especially women and children who resort to crossing the sea in search of a sanctuary elsewhere.

a register of drowned bodies

i.

The boats of grief. The boats of drowned
immigrants surfacing on the sea. On the frail
body of water there are waves heavy with the
last prayers of the dead. There is a map of drowning.
The map carries the ruins of dreams, the memories
of things lost to the sea. Beneath the sea, there are
bits of bones that belong to unburied dead. How do
we trace the depth of water that claims our loved ones?
How do we track the footprints of the drowned on water?

ii.

Today, the book of history opens to a page darkened
by the gory event of Igbo landing: in 1803, 75 Igbo slaves
were crammed on a ship named *Wanderer*, on a ship
that ferried them to Dunbar Creek where their cries
cleaved the air, where they rose, like a tide, against
their captors; where they sung their songs of victory
and marched into the sea, their bodies merging with
water, their bodies dissolving into songs.

iii.

In the register of drowned bodies, there are forgotten
children. They are children who will not be able
to throw a kite into the air, nor race across the streets
with paper-made fans again. They will not be able
to pick seashells or watch birds traverse the sky.
Tonight, there are women holding a vigil on behalf
of all their missing loved ones. They weep for the sea
and the residues of drowned bodies. They weep for the
dreams perished at sea; dreams wrecked by the tide
of water. Tonight, there are boats of grief. There are
ships on water, ships reminding us of black slaves
ferried across the dark passage of the sea in slavery.

CONCHA MÉNDEZ

Translated by Harriet Truscott from Spanish

Concha Méndez was a lover of water and the sea throughout her life: sea images recur endless as waves within her poetry. A champion swimmer as a girl, despite the restrictions placed on women in Spain at that time, water became a symbol of strength and of rebellion in her writing. The sea offered her the opportunity to escape the expectations of her wealthy family, and she took a cargo boat to England and beyond. After the Spanish Civil War and her exile to Mexico, however, the ocean also became emblematic of her separation from her country. These two poems, both published in her 1944 collection *Sombras y Sueños* (Shadows and Dreams), show these very different aspects of the sea in her writing.

This Must Be My Last Loss

This must be my last loss,
I repeat each time
grief rips apart the sky
leaving me weeping.

I don't want to learn
that we are each a sea
where losses come as waves
breaking, always breaking.

Rest

I don't want rest. I want
to live, head spinning,
in the sun. I'll sleep late
later, when a stone
rests in the shade.

But now I want to breathe
and be and make and be
remade. I want to leave
a long wake in the water—
restless, unafraid.

NADIA LÓPEZ GARCÍA AKA NADIA ÑUU SAVI

Translated by Gabriela Ramirez-Chavez and Whitney DeVos
from Spanish

Nadia López García AKA Nadia Ñuu Savi publishes bilingually in
Spanish and the Tu'un Savi language, spoken in the Mixteca Alta region
of Oaxaca, Mexico. Her poem 'The Way of the Deer' takes as its subject
a communal ritual observed by the Ñuu Savi community in Nadia's
hometown of Tlaxiaco. In times of hardship, it was once common for
a group of respected leaders to set off in search of a deer, a sign of
wisdom and a good omen. Only local Ñuu Savi men who are married
and have children may participate in the search, which can take up to a
week. The act works to consolidate long-standing bonds: both between
men on the journey and the women who make the preparations and
look after the community in their absence. Today, mass migration and
its devastating economic consequences have made it increasingly
difficult for a dwindling number of eligible men to give up several
days' work. And deer have become harder to find, their habitat
encroached upon by highway construction, narcoviolence, and the
effects of climate change. Nadia approaches the ritual from a feminist
perspective, wondering if the 'way of the deer' will ultimately go
extinct because those available to carry it out cannot participate. The
poem proposes that Ñuu Savi women—barred from participating, yet
responsible for transmitting Tu'un Savi to the next generation—be
seen as the deer. That is, perhaps the search for communal wisdom
leads inward as much as beyond. At the poem's end, the speaker
imagines taking the journey herself.

The Way of the Deer

That night, I wept at the ash in your mouth,
the water pounding in your head.
I uncovered night's mantle
and saw the way of the deer.
Its black eyes howled the pain
of men like you,
Father.

Men who bound their hearts
and forgot the sound of rain,
the sound of their own language.

Today
I follow the way of the deer,
return to our pueblo and search for
the tree root that brings us rain,
sacred rain we know is coming
when the ants begin their march.

Father,
I have seen the way of the deer
its steps
hold a hidden truth:

The rain will spring up once more,
        before long
the Ñuu Savi people
will rise from the water
and our blood,
        our word,
                will flourish,
                        yet again.

REVIEWS

Varieties of Space

Dear Beloved Humans by Grzegorz Wróblewski (translated
by Piotr Gwiazda), Diálogos Books, 2023
Review by Dawid Mobolaji

An orangutan legally recognised as a person, a bedwetting
astronomer with a fear of long distances, Emperor Hadrian making
penis jokes over smoked mackerel. These are some of the weird
and wonderful inhabitants of Grzegorz Wróblewski's *Dear Beloved
Humans*—a mosaic of clearly imagined, absurdly funny tableaus—
translated by Piotr Gwiazda. Spanning four decades of the poet's
creative output (from the early 1980s until now), the collection
is equally broad in its content, oscillating between Denmark,
Poland, Japan and California, between the present, the ancient
and mediaeval pasts, and arguably the future. What could connect
such variety?

In his translator's preface, Gwiazda proposes the poems' subject
matter may be 'almost secondary to the acts of close looking and
careful listening they [record]'. Indeed, like a photographer toying
with their lenses, Wróblewski craftily engineers perspectives. Poems
in *Dear Beloved Humans* often function as distorting mirrors—or
'Varieties of Space' as one is titled—where minute details swell to
extraordinary proportions. The speaker in 'Fast Trip' celebrates
finding a fly in his bed, as it gives him something to observe instead
of 'the single black hair stuck to the fluffy rug [which] has ceased
to entertain [him]'. We see the world through eyes much different
than our own, quite literally, in 'Dead Cod':

They stare as the sweating pedestrians
complain with disgust:
Such revolting fish... Why hasn't anyone
gouged out their eyes?

This is an example of Wróblewski's brilliant, terse humour hinging
on vivid images. He folds them on themselves, like impossible Escher
drawings, to demonstrate the paradoxes of human experience. The way
of looking in this poem—the fish eyes—becomes conflict in itself. The
watchful cod also illustrate one of the collection's most stark features.
Despite the seemingly anthropocentric title, animals frequently take
the centre stage—moralising spiders and cross-bearing lemurs are but
a few examples—while poems such as 'I Gathered Everyone' take a
more radical, post-humanist approach to personhood:

I gathered everyone –
the wire-rimmed glasses
the yellow wallpaper and the linocut hanging on the wall [...]

Moving through the collection, existential questions and ideas of the
apocalypse start to bubble beneath the comedy. The opening and titular
poem sets us up for this. It stands as not only a bold establishment of
the book's relationship with the reader, defiant in its simplicity, but also
an elastic frame which successfully facilitates reading the collection
as a coherent whole, despite its temporospatial wingspan:

I have a message for you
my name is Grzegorz Wróblewski
my father's name was Roman
and my grandfather's name was Józef
This is my message for humans

The 'message'—originally delivered by Wróblewski in a YouTube video and never before appearing in print (Gwiazda, 2018)—reads like an SOS signal, somehow final and interplanetary. Indeed, we see spaceships and cosmonauts in the collection. Wróblewski's allusions to humanity on the cusp of collapse engages *Dear Beloved Humans* in very current anxieties around the Anthropocene.

Poems in the first half of the collection tackle this from a more depressive position. Watching the 'uninspiring' weather outside, the speaker in 'Melancholia' plays by twisting the fingernail of his 'bleeding finger [...] like a wax crayon'—reminiscent of the injured thumb and the associated spiralling introspection of Sylvia Plath's 'Cut'. Caught between talking pigeons and these moments of claustrophobic anticipation, the book reveals the existential uncertainty at its core: 'waiting for war is the worst'. The precarity contrasts the settings—names like Christianshavn, Ørstedsparken and Hareskov activate our notions of the Scandinavian utopia in the background—reminding us of Wróblewski's context as an émigré artist.

When considering the origin of his poetry, a cursory online search may suggest he belongs to the so-called *Brulion* Generation. *Brulion* was a literary magazine published in Poland from 1988 to 1999 in which time it published many of the greatest Polish writers, including Wróblewski. However, as pointed out in *Polish Literature in Transformation*, edited by Ursula Phillips, simply being a poet born in the 1960s was enough to be considered part of the *Brulion* collective which, in reality, contained writers of many different styles and backgrounds. For instance, the Nobel Prize winner Olga Tokarczuk is named alongside Wróblewski as a representative of the *Brulion* movement.

Looking for a key to *Dear Beloved Humans*, we can consider instead Wróblewski's admiration of the Objectivist poets, Charles Reznikoff and William Carlos Williams. We see similar sincerity and clarity of vision from Wróblewski alongside excellent command of form in 'You Can't Expand on This Poem, You Can Only Copy It from the Screen':

> Poetry contest topic:
> *The power of the rosary.*

The above poem really does function as an object. Its meaning emerges from the title instructing us to move in one way, while its body would have us respond differently. The poem 'Assistens Kirkegård' is made entirely of tombstone epitaphs, while 'Sandra's Blanket' mimics a web page with pesky pop-ups.

Wróblewski thus constructs his poems like machinery, where words and spaces between them function as gears, often over just a few lines. This concision, somewhat a hallmark of the case-rich Polish language and key to Wróblewski's nonchalant colloquialism, no doubt poses a challenge in translation. Gwiazda finds witty solutions. The astronaut in 'The Moon' is rather unimpressed upon reaching his destination: 'Been there. Just craters.' The first sentence might hint at the English phrase *been there, done that* which, although not present in Polish, fits the speaker's attitude perfectly. As such, Gwiazda works to firmly root the collection in its target language.

Dear Beloved Humans is a cackle in the face of an absurd, indifferent, almost finished world—a grey afterparty. When writing about animals, Wróblewski avoids the traps of dichotomies and misanthropy. He conveys disillusionment with simple, romantic solutions to the human world in crisis—an acute awareness that modern humanity is an entirely separate and unprecedented entity for which there is no clear answer. While he might 'dislike the idea of the poet-as-prophet or poet-as-witness', Wróblewski certainly expounds poetry's value. Given his declarative opening, is it poetry as communication? In any case, he sets its value over ordinary words concretely, going as far as providing an exchange rate, in the poem '¡Viva España!':

My rates (per source word):
standard translation ES <> PL 0,07 euro

Poetry translation 0,25 euro
(per source word)

Linguistic Dissidence

A Tower Built Downwards by Yang Lian (translated by
Brian Holton), Bloodaxe Books, 2023
  Review by Jenny He

Solid gold surveillance cameras hang amidst handcuffs and dripping
chains, against a black backdrop, on the cover of Yang Lian's latest
collection *A Tower Built Downwards*. The artwork, created especially
for the book by his long-time friend Ai Weiwei, is a social critique of
contemporary China, where more than 600 million CCTV cameras
monitor the day-to-day activities of the population. A population which
ranges from the labouring migrant workers who huddle together in
dormitories of half-finished sky-scrapers, to the vastly wealthy business
tycoons chauffeured silently through Beijing in shining black Bentleys.

Living in exile since the 1989 student protests in Tiananmen,
Yang Lian's work will undoubtedly be read as political, and this is
certainly upheld in the introduction by Ai Weiwei, naming Yang
Lian a 'battle-hardened soldier'. Indeed, at a recent reading from the
work at London's Coronet Theatre, one of the poems performed was
'Poems on Turning Back History *for Hong Kong*'. Many of the poems
come with a date, conferring on them the status of witness testimony
to the horrors they recount.

Although the text contains numerous references to huge political
events—the pandemic, the Snowden affair, the invasion of Ukraine—
Yang Lian's poetry is also an exposition of how national policies become
personal tragedies. 'Anti-Requiem', written for his brother who died four
days after the CCP lifted Covid restrictions, is a reminder of the personal
relationship we each have with large-scale political events. The response
to the poem, covertly circulated in China, has been one of recognition
for a grief which has largely been concealed from public view.

The most disturbingly moving poem of the collection, 'Green Grass Offering (for Deng Shiping)' memorialises

> a teacher at Xinhuang No. 1 High School who refused to sign off on shoddy building work for the headmaster's relatives ... his bones were found four metres under the school sports ground, hogtied, his hands behind his back.

We often talk of such 'minor atrocities' as a footnote in history—Deng Shiping's story is a literal footnote to the poem—as though they were unimportant; but Yang Lian's explanation of the monograph to his poem is precisely because it is otherwise.

To say that this book is 'only' political, would however, be doing Yang Lian a massive disservice. The poems reference themselves, each other, and a myriad of elements, forming a Joycean web of intertextuality. *A Tower Built Downwards* is the transgression of language.

This is most strongly exemplified in the longer poems 'Labyrinth', plotting a complex maze of references to ensnare the reader, and the titular poem 'A Tower Built Downwards'—a poem so saturated in references that it threatens to collapse under its own weight. The latter poem is almost entirely unpunctuated, except for a few question marks, and any pause you choose to provide at a line break in this

page   after   page

of tiny close-written words

The incessant torrent of language, 'a terror of black words on white paper', is demanding of the reader. In the second part of the poem, mourning for his father blends with Dali-esque melting clocks 'dripping then or now?' and Wordsworth's 'daffodils thousands of miles away'.

Similarly surreal is the poem 'Orwell's New Year *A Verse Drama*', a conversation between characters Translator, Orwell, Winston, Julia, and Ghost. They are all introduced at the beginning with a single line bio, that links them to the text of the novel *Nineteen Eighty Four*, followed by a stage direction: '*with solo cello, modern dance, art installation*'.

The construction of such a poem is reminiscent of Tom Stoppard's play 'Travesties', which recontextualises Lenin, James Joyce, and Tristan Tzara in an imagined meeting in Zurich, though Yang Lian writes in the penultimate stanza that it is 'a script that can't be performed'. Certainly, it could not be in China, where this is one of the poems that remains unpublished.

The form of the poem is also a play on intertextuality:

<blockquote>
extracts

2021 the original of 1984
</blockquote>

as the contemporary context is received as inspiration for a fiction written in the past. Each character takes their turn at delivering a stanza, usually of eight lines and of a regular metre (in the Chinese they are all eight lines), which loosely reference the novel, as they consider our own historical context in a convergence of moments from the cultural revolution through to the advent of social media.

A key theme of the poem is the politicisation of language, and the insidious way this has infiltrated our identities, as we perform our existence on social media.

<blockquote>
we who are added to a fiction   are powerless

as a fiction   we who are reduced to imitations
</blockquote>

Technology can censor and halt communication, preventing the spread of content considered disruptive to the authorities; but, in the line 'self-censored Wechat is blocked as usual' Yang Lian highlights the availability of free and instant communication only serves as a placebo of freedom, when the ideology is so ingrained that users inhibit their own expressions.

Yang Lian readily admits this is a 'difficult book', and Brian Holton's translation is a masterpiece, which must have left the latter completely exhausted. Particularly anxiety-inducing for Holton must have been the thread of comments throughout 'Orwell's New Year' on the nature of translation. The technique is reminiscent of Derrida's essay 'Surviving On Borderlines', written specifically for translation into English, and the footnoted section of the essay makes direct remarks addressing the prospective translator and their translation choices.

This close working relationship is the result of a thirty-year partnership, which has enabled a cooperation whereby Yang Lian gives detailed feedback on each line of the draft translation, before Brian Holton revises the work until both are satisfied with the translation, so given the line 'a translation's victory is never to be revised' he must have discovered towards the end of this process that the rules of the game were against him from the outset.

These lines are almost a private joke between the pair, as Yang Lian has a great respect for translation, describing it as 'the third language'. The special status afforded by the hybridity of the translation is intensified in this edition, which includes several poems that cannot be officially published in mainland China, due to censorship laws: *A Tower Built Downwards* exists in a full and revised text, which the original mainland Chinese publication is not permitted to embody. It is a work of both political and linguistic dissidence.

NOTES ON CONTRIBUTORS

BETH HICKLING-MOORE is a literary translator, writer and educator. She translates from Portuguese, Spanish and Italian, with an interest in underrepresented majority world voices, such as women from Lusophone Africa.

CINDY JUYOUNG OK is the author of *Ward Toward* (Yale University Press, 2024). She teaches poetry at Kenyon College.

CONCHA MÉNDEZ (1898–1986) was a Spanish writer, editor and member of the 'Hatless Women', a group of radical '20s artists. Much of her life was spent in exile in Mexico.

DAISY ROCKWELL is a Hindi-Urdu to English translator and artist. She is the winner of the 2021 International Booker Prize for her translation of Geetanjali Shree's *Tomb of Sand*.

DARCY PAQUET is a translator and film scholar who has lived in Seoul since 1997. He has translated the subtitles for many Korean films including *Parasite* and *Decision to Leave*.

DAWID MOBOLAJI is a Polish-Nigerian literary translator, writer and medical doctor based in London. He was selected as one of the ALTA Travel Fellows for 2023.

DERK WYNAND is a German-born Canadian, author of several books of poems and translations, including two of Dorothea Grünzweig's poems. He taught at the University of Victoria, BC, until 2004.

DOROTHEA GRÜNZWEIG, German poet and translator, has lived in Finland since 1989. Her work includes seven collections of poems and a book of translations of G.M. Hopkins. The latest of her many honours is the Kurt Sigel Prize, awarded by the German Centre of PEN.

EMILY GRAHAM is an MFA candidate in Literary Translation at the University of Iowa. Her translations of Baros have been featured in *Asymptote*, the *New England Review*, *Fence*, and more.

ERIC ABALAJON's translations have appeared in *Asymptote, Mercury Firs, Four Way Review, The Polyglot,* and *Exchanges: Journal of Literary Translation.* He lives near Iloilo City, Philippines.

GABRIELA RAMIREZ-CHAVEZ is a Seattle-based poet and translator born to Guatemalan immigrants. Her translations have been featured on NPR and in POETRY, *World Literature Today, BOMB, Asymptote,* and elsewhere.

GONCA ÖZMEN (Burdur, 1982), poet and translator based in Istanbul has published three collections of poetry in Turkish and has been widely translated. She is currently translating Sylvia Plath's *Collected Poems.*

GUILLERMO RUIZ PLAZA is an acclaimed author and poet from Bolivia. He's published two poetry collections and authored novels like *Dias Detenidos* and *El Hombre Tocado de Viento.*

HAGIWARA SAKUTARO (1886–1942) revolutionised Japanese poetry with his intense focus on emotion and experience, and his visceral imagery. He wrote that 'a poem is a living, working psychology.'

HARRIET TRUSCOTT is a poet and translator, currently living in the (rainy) north of Spain. Her own poetry appears in journals including *The Dark Horse, Oxford Poetry* and *Magma.*

JAKU MATA is a cultural worker that resides in Dumaguete and Iloilo. He is the author of the chapbook *Lugar Lang* (Lomboy Press, 2023).

JENNIFER HAYASHIDA is a poet, translator, and artist based in Stockholm. Her translations between Swedish and English include work by Athena Farrokhzad, Don Mee Choi, Iman Mohammed, and Kim Hyesoon.

JENNY HE is a first-year doctoral researcher in translation and transcultural studies at the University of Warwick. In her free time, she enjoys drawing, photography, and walking in Wales.

JOAQUÍN GAVILANO, a Bolivian translator and writer, serves as an editor for *The Arkansas International* and attends the University of Arkansas MFA program. He received a PEN/Heim grant in 2023.

JOHN GREENING (b.1954) is an editor and author of over twenty collections. Recent books include his Goethe, *Nightwalker's Song,* and *The Interpretation of Owls: Selected Poems 1977–2022* (Baylor, ed. Gardner).

JOHN NEWTON WEBB's poems and translations are widely published. You can read his work and mini-essays on Japanese poetry at johnnewtonwebb.blogspot.com. He lives in Sapporo, Japan, where he is a pastor.

KATRINA NAOMI's poetry collections have won an Authors' Foundation Award and Saboteur Award, and she is a recipient of the Keats-Shelley Prize. Katrina's forthcoming collection, *Battery Rocks,* is due in July 2024 from Seren.

KIM HYESOON has published fourteen poetry collections and was the first woman to win the Kim Suyoung, Midang, Daesan literary awards in South Korea. Her international honors include the Griffin Poetry Prize from Canada and the Cikada Prize from Sweden, and her books have been translated into several languages. Kim was a creative writing professor at the Seoul Institute of the Arts for many years and has a Ph.D. in Korean Literature from Konkuk University.

KIM SEON-HYANG was born in Daejeon, South Korea in 1966, and has published two collections of poetry to date: *The Front of a Woman* (2016) and *F-Grade Movie* (2020). This is the first poem of hers to be published in English.

KINNARI SARAIYA (born in Bombay, India, in 1998), is an artist-curator, writer and folk fancer based in the UK. Her practice utilises ancient, sensorial and trans-media storytelling formats that transcend visual imperiality to reveal a hybrid, decolonial and feminist ecstatic truth.

LAUREN SHAPIRO is the author of two collections of poetry, *Arena* and *Easy Math.* Her full length translation of Zaira Pacheco's book, *Waking in the Desert,* will be published by Eulalia Books. She is an associate professor of English at Carnegie Mellon University.

LAWRENCE SCHIMEL (New York, 1971) has translated over 150 books, into Spanish or English, including work by Danez Smith, Maggie Nelson, Koleka Putuma, Trifonia Melibea Obono, and Agnès Agboton.

LINDA MARIA BAROS is a poet, translator, and publisher whose work has been published in translation in 41 countries. Winner of the prestigious Apollinaire Prize, Baros lives in Paris.

MALLIKA SENGUPTA (1960–2011) was a Bengali poet, political activist and academic. Known for her 'unapologetically political poetry', she was actively involved with the cause of gender justice and other social issues. She died at only 51 following a battle with breast cancer.

MAMATA NANDA authored the first official Bengali translation of Maya Angelou's collected poems. She has been published in numerous international anthologies and magazines including *MPT*. Her next book is a Bengali translation of Sylvia Plath.

MARIE-LOUISE EYRES: Poems in *Shearsman, Acumen, Agenda, Stand, Poetry, Portland Review;* Bridport, Bedford, Ginkgo & Live Canon anthologies. Pamphlets by Maverick Duck, Ghost City, Alien Buddha & Finishing Line.

MAY MORALES DOLIS grew up in Marinduque and now resides in Bacoor, Cavite. She is the author of the chapbook *Ayon Kay Kid Talaba* (2023).

MELITA MATSINHE is an artist, musician and poet from Mozambique. She studied music in Havana, where she deepened her sense for aesthetics, dance and poetry, exploring ideas such as music, religion and divinity. *Ignição dos Sonhos* is her first poetry collection.

MERIMA DIZDAREVIĆ is an artist and writer based in Malmö, Sweden. Born in Yugoslavia in 1983 (Bosnia and Herzegovina), her practice is multidisciplinary and multilingual, encompassing poetry, criticism, and performance.

NAAMA JUNG has a Bachelors degree in English and French Literature, and a Masters degree in Journalism from NYU. She has published three poetry books in Hebrew, *Beings, The Lamb Of Honey* and *Past Continuous.* She has one daughter, Gali.

NADIA LÓPEZ GARCÍA AKA NADIA ÑUU SAVI is the author of five poetry books. Her work has been translated into eight languages and was awarded the 2021 Luis Cardoza y Aragón Mesoamerican Poetry Prize.

NEIL P. DOHERTY (Dublin, 1972) is a translator of Turkish poetry. His translations have been published in various journals. He is currently at work on collections by Gonca Özmen and Behçet Necatigil.

NIALL O'GALLAGHER is the author of three collections of Gaelic poetry published by CLÀR and of *Fuaimean Gràidh / The Sounds of Love: Selected Poems* (Francis Boutle, 2023). He is currently translating poems from the Catalan of Josep Carner, supported by the Institut Ramon Llull. He lives in Ayrshire, Scotland.

NNADI SAMUEL (he/him/his) holds a B.A in English & literature from the University of Benin. Author of *Nature knows a little about Slave Trade* selected by Tate.N.Oquendo (Sundress Publication, 2023). A 3x Best of the Net, and 7x Pushcart Nominee. He tweets @Samuelsamba10.

PALOMA CHEN (Alicante, 1997) is a Spanish poet and journalist. She has published the poetry collections *Invocación a las mayorías silenciosas* (Letraversal) and the multilingual app Shanshui Pixel Scenes 山水像素场景, featuring her poetry combined with work of pixel artists @neopixel_art, @erien.strf, @waneella & @abueloretrowave.

RAINER MARIA RILKE (1875–1926) remains the most popular and widely translated German-language poet in English-speaking countries. The 170+ poems in the two volumes of his *New Poems* (1907 and 1908) were written under the influence of Rodin, chiefly in Paris.

RASAQ MALIK GBOLAHAN is a Nigerian poet, essayist, and translator. He is the co-founder of *Atelewo* (www.atelewo.org), the first indigenous online journal devoted to publishing literary work written in the Yorùbá language.

S. VIJAYALAKSHMI is a teacher by profession, actively engaged in the Tamil literary field, penning poetry and articles on literary and social issues. She has contributed poems and essays to several mainstream and alternate Tamil magazines, and has to her credit four published books of poetry, one book of short stories, and two collections of essays.

SAKTHI JOTHI is a social worker by occupation, and is the author of thirteen books of poetry and two collections of essays, and a recipient of numerous awards. She is also the founder of Sri Sakthi Social, Economic and Educational Welfare Trust that focuses on promoting the welfare of youth and women through sustainable socio-economic development.

SODÏQ OYÈKÀNMÍ is a poet, dramaturg and translator. A 2022/23 Poetry Translation Centre (UK) UNDERTOW Fellow, he won the 2022 Lagos / London Poetry Competition. Find him on Twitter/X @sodiqoyekan.

SUN KYOUNG YOON is an Associate Professor of literary translation at the Hankuk University of Foreign Studies. She has published articles on poetry translation and feminist translation in international journals.

TARAN SPALDING-JENKIN is an award-winning poet, performer, translator, and native Kernewek speaker exploring disability, home and queerness. Their debut pamphlet *Health Hireth* was published by Broken Sleep Books in 2023.

THILA VARGHESE lives in Canada, where she works part-time during the academic year as a Senior Writing Advisor at Western University. Her translations of Tamil literary works have been published in international magazines and journals.

VAIBHAV SHARMA is a Hindi poet and Hindi-English translator from India. His translations have appeared in *Out of Print*, *WWB*. His first translated book comes out Feb 2024.

WHITNEY DEVOS is a scholar, translator, and 2022 NEA Translation Fellow. Her current work focuses on lenguas originarias, the autochthonous languages of the Americas. She lives in Mexico City.

ZAIRA PACHECO is a poet and critic with a doctorate in literature from the University of Barcelona. She is the author of two books of poetry and two essay collections. She is a professor of language and literature in the Spanish Department at the Univerity of Puerto Rico, Río Piedras.